Little Book of

Brittany Nightshade

Table of Contents

Merry Meet!

The Little Book of White Magic Spells is a compact grimoire brimming with beginner-friendly white magic rituals, perfect for both newcomers and experienced practitioners seeking fresh inspiration in the realm of light work.

Whether you choose to adapt these spells to craft your unique rituals or follow them as they are, always remember that the true magic resides within you. There are no strict rules; it's all about channeling your intentions. Personalization strengthens the magic, so feel free to modify any ritual to align with what resonates with you. If a ritual mentions a specific deity that doesn't resonate with you, substitute it with one that empowers your practice.

Your magical abilities will flourish through meditation and practice, so don't fear mistakes or rush towards ideals of perfection. It's all about you and your energies. I extend my blessings and best wishes as you continue to walk your unique path. - Brittany Nightshade

Circle Casting

Casting a circle is a fundamental aspect of many witchcraft traditions, serving as a ritual method to create a sacred space for magical workings. The process begins with understanding its purpose: to provide protection, concentrate energy, and establish a connection with spiritual realms. The selection and cleansing of the space are crucial first steps, where a practitioner might choose a quiet area and cleanse it using methods like smudging or sprinkling salt water.

Gathering tools and symbols is a personal choice, and one might include items such as a wand, athame, candles, crystals, or incense, along with representations of the elements or deities. The actual casting of the circle involves grounding oneself, a practice of visualizing roots extending into the earth for stability and focus. The circle is then drawn, either physically or mentally, envisioning a barrier of protection and energy. This act is often accompanied by the calling of the quarters, an invocation of the cardinal directions and their associated elements.

If the practice includes working with deities or spiritual energies, this is the time to invite them respectfully, clearly stating the purpose of their presence. Raising energy within the circle can be achieved through various means such as chanting, dancing, or drumming, focusing on the intent of the magical work to be done.

The ritual work, be it spellcasting, divination, meditation, or other practices, is performed within the boundaries of the circle. The importance of maintaining focus and respect for the space and energies at play cannot be overstated.

Closing the circle is as important as its creation. It involves thanking and releasing any invoked deities or energies, dismissing the elements and directions often in the reverse order of their invocation, and then opening the circle, either visualizing its energy dissipating or being absorbed back into the earth. Grounding oneself again is crucial to avoid feeling unbalanced or drained.

The beauty of this practice lies in its adaptability. Practitioners are encouraged to personalize the process, incorporating symbols, chants, or rituals that resonate with them, making the circle as elaborate or as simple as they wish. This flexibility, however, comes with a responsibility to approach the practice with respect and a willingness to continuously learn, understanding the historical and cultural contexts of the elements incorporated.

Elemental Circle Casting

With your wand, or other tool, in your dominant hand point towards the east side of the circle and say the following.

"I call upon the Guardian of the East, Element of Air, to watch over this sacred space."

Envision the Guardian appearing in the east, bow to acknowledge the Guardian and turn to the south. With hand extended say the following.

"I call upon the Guardian of the South, Element of Fire, to watch over this sacred space."

Envision the Guardian, bow to acknowledge him and turn to the west. With hand extended say the following.

"I call upon the Guardian of the West, Element of Water, to watch over this sacred space."

As you envision the arrival of the Guardian, bow in respect and turn to the North. With Arm still extended, say the following.

"I call upon the Guardian of the North, Element of Earth, to watch over this sacred space."

Raise your hand up into the air and say the following.

"I call upon the spirit to protect this space, as I will, the circle is cast."

With this your circle has been cast. Once you are you done you may close the circle by simply raising your hand and thanking the elements, drop your hand to conclude the ritual and close the circle.

Sage Cleansing (Smudging)

You can cleanse just about anything with the smoke from sage. This is either done with a sage stick (smudge stick) or by burning sage in an incense burner. Sage has powerful cleansing properties and can be used to cleanse your home, altar space, jewelry, crystals, candles and any other ritual tool or object. Sage can also be used to cleanse yourself. Other common incense used for cleansing are myrrh and dragons blood but I typically use sage.

To cleanse your home set your intention to cleanse and light your sage and allow it to burn out and smolder. Carry the sage throughout the house and allow the smoke to flow into the rooms, pay special attention to mirrors, hallways, and other high traffic areas. As you do this you can say prayer to the goddess or an incantation to better focus your intention.

To cleanse an object do the same thing, set your intention and light your sage and run the object through the smoke. If the object is large, take the sage and move it around the object letting the smoke envelope it.

To cleanse yourself light your sage and allow it to burn out, take the smoke with your hands and direct it around your body. "Wash" your hands, face, body, legs, etc. with the smoke. Do this with the intent of cleansing and purification.

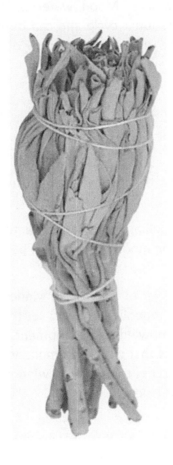

Moon Water

Moon water is a versatile tool that's used in many spiritual practices. Moon water is imbued with the energy of the lunar cycle and can be made during any phase of the moon, each phase offering its unique qualities.

You will need:

A clear jar

Water

A window that receives moonlight

Begin by filling your jar with water. Choose a clear jar to allow the moon's rays to fully permeate the water.

Place the jar of water on a windowsill where it will be bathed in moonlight. As you set the jar down take a moment acknowledge the moment, focusing on the lunar energies that will be permeating the water. If you don't have access to a moonlit window you can always take the jar outside.

Leave the jar on the windowsill overnight, allowing it to soak up the moon's energy.

Different moon phases can impart different qualities to the water:

New Moon: Ideal for new beginnings, setting intentions, and manifestation.

Waxing Moon: Suitable for growth, attraction, and building things.

Full Moon: Perfect for healing, charging spiritual tools, and amplification of energies.

Waning Moon: Great for release, banishing, and clearing negative energies.

In the morning, retrieve your jar. Your moon water is now charged with the lunar energy of that particular phase. Seal the jar with a lid to preserve its energy. You can use moon water in various ways, such as in rituals, to water plants, in baths, or as a cleansing spray.

Remember, each lunar cycle offers a unique energy, so you can repeat this ritual monthly, aligning your intentions with the specific phase of the moon to harness its specific energies.

Sea Water

Sea water is water that's been imbued with the energies of both the earth and the sea. It is frequently used for purification, protection, and as a tool in various rituals and spells, symbolizing the cleansing and healing properties of water combined with the grounding and nurturing aspects of earth. Additionally, sea water can be used to consecrate spaces, tools, and in the creation of sacred circles, harnessing its natural power to enhance spiritual practices. If you don't have access to natural sea water you can always make your own.

You will need:

A glass jar
Water
Sea salt
A seashell (optional)

Start by filling your jar with the water. This water serves as the base of your Sea Water, representing purity and fluidity. Next, add a generous amount of sea salt to the water. As you do this, think about the grounding properties of the earth and the cleansing power of the sea. If you're using a seashell, place it inside or next to the jar.

Once your jar is prepared, hold it in your hands or place your hands on the vessel. Close your eyes and focus on the elements of water and earth. Feel their presence and their intrinsic qualities; the fluidity, intuition, and emotional depth of water, and the stability, grounding, and nurturing aspects of earth.

Say the following invocation:

"Elements of water and earth, I call upon you in this sacred ritual. With sea salt from the depths of the earth and water, the source of life, I combine your energies. Bless this Sea Water with your essence. May it be imbued with your purity, strength, and wisdom. As these elements merge, let this water become a vessel of your balanced powers, for cleansing, protection, and connection to the natural world."

Visualize a gentle energy radiating from your hands into the jar, charging the water with the combined powers of water and earth. Feel a sense of harmony and balance as these elements unite.

Your Sea Water is now ready. You can use it immediately or store it for future use. It can be used for a number of things, such as cleansing spaces, protection, anointing, or as an offering in rituals. Remember to thank the elements for their contribution to your practice.

Invocation of Hecate

Hecate is the Greek Goddess of Witchcraft and magic. She holds the keys to the underworld and can protect against the spirits of the nether just as she can send them to attack. She's known as a liminal goddess, meaning she freely crosses between realms of Earth, Heaven, Hell and can walk the veil that separates the three. She is as strict as she is kind, so do not cross her. She can bring along death as she can life. Hecate is known as the Triple Moon Goddess and holds dominion over the Earth, Heavens, and Sea and wields immeasurable power as a daughter of Titans and mother of gods.

If you acquire her favor, she will shield you against harm and bring along creativity, wisdom, and guidance. She is darkness. She is everything. But do not fear her. Hecate is the crone, the mother of all witches. As you develop a relationship with her you will find that the knowledge and wisdom needed to bring forth light resides in the mysteries and blessings of the dark.

It helps if you are in a meditative state when calling on a deity, but you do not have to be. It would help if you have one of your deity's symbols, for instance, some of Hecate's symbols are the moon, keys, black, silver, darkness, crossroads, the number three and dogs (it's said the sound of hounds sometimes heralds her arrival). Hecate is easiest to call on at night. Since she represents each phase of the moon, it doesn't have to be at a certain time of month. Make sure to hold the symbol and focus on it. If it is something that you cannot hold (like the moon or darkness), then just focus on it wherever it may be.

Clear your mind and let the image fill your mind, then begin to relax. Concentrate on your energy connecting with darkness, feel your energies being aligned with hers and say the following.

"Hecate, Mother of Darkness, I call upon you!

Goddess of Night, protect me with your arcane power!

Grant me the sight to see through the veil and attain the wisdom you grant!

Maiden of thresholds and crossroads, surround me in your darkness so that I can bring forth my light!

Dark Mother! I honor you now and forever! By the power of the Triple Moon!

Hail Hecate! Hail Hecate! Hail Hecate! "

Pray to Hecate regularly, I normally hold a ritual on the new moon and give thanks and offerings on a daily basis. Cherish the bond you have with her as her grace will be a blessing that will protect and lead you through the void.

Bonding with a Familiar

A familiar is an animal or nature spirit that you can bond with that can assist you in your practice, familiars can lend you their energies and protect against malevolent forces. Some bonds happen naturally but you can also perform a ritual to attempt create a familiar bond.

Embrace the animal or envision the spirit you wish to be bond with and say the following:

"A bond to be made in (god, goddess, or entities) name,
I ask for your assistance,
Keep me safe from all that'd harm,
And counter all resistance.
Together we can do great things,
No matter what the 'morrow brings."

Meditate on the connection between your spirit and theirs, you will feel the connection when it's made. If the spell didn't work keep in mind that not every spirit wants to or is ready to be your familiar and you stand a much greater chance if you have already built a connection with spirit you are trying to enlist. As you grow in experience you might find that familiars might call to you and your ability to bond with them will grow.

Pentacle Ward Spell

This spell is designed to create a protective ward around your home or a specific space, invoking the guidance and protection of the goddess Hecate.

You will need:

A sage smudge stick

A key

A pentacle (pendant or drawn symbol)

Begin by lighting the sage smudge stick and allow its smoke to fill the area you wish to protect. Hold the key in your dominant hand and the pentacle in your other hand. Walk around the perimeter of the space, envisioning a protective barrier being formed by the smoke. As you walk, chant the following invocation to Hecate:

"Hecate, guardian at the crossroads, hear my plea,
With this key, I lock away all negativity.
By the pentacle's enduring strength, I draw a protective ring,
Sage purify, this space I now bring.
Ward this place, safe and secure,
Under your watch, harm shall not endure."

Visualize Hecate's energy surrounding the area, strengthening the barrier you've created. Once you have walked the full perimeter, place the key in a somewhere within the warded space. The spell is now complete and your space is surrounded by a protective ward under the watchful guidance of Hecate.

Oceanic Protection Jar

This ritual creates a portable jar imbued with protective ocean energies, invoking the blessings of the sea goddess Amphitrite.

You will need:
A small glass jar with a lid
A sea shell
A quartz crystal
Sea salt
Water
Sand (optional)

Begin by filling the jar halfway with water. Add a pinch of sea salt, stirring gently to dissolve it. If you're using sand, add a layer to the bottom of the jar before adding water. Place the sea shell and quartz crystal into the jar, envisioning them as conductors of the ocean's vast and protective energy.

Hold the jar in your hands and close your eyes, focusing your mind on the vastness of the ocean and the protective embrace of its waters. Chant the following invocation to Amphitrite:

"Amphitrite, queen of the sea's endless flow,
In this jar, your protective powers bestow.
With shell, quartz, salt, and water clear,
Guard against harm, both far and near.
As the tides ebb and flow with grace,
Surround this space with your safe embrace."

Visualize the goddess Amphitrite's energy flowing into the jar, filling it with a bright, protective light. Seal the jar tightly with its lid. The protection jar is now charged with the protective energies of the ocean and the blessing of Amphitrite. Carry it with you for personal protection or place it in a chosen space to safeguard the area.

Goal Accomplishment Jar Ritual

This ritual focuses on manifesting a specific goal or aspiration, using a combination of potent symbolic elements to create a charged jar.

You will need:

A small jar with a lid or cork

Graveyard dirt

Pepper (any type)

A red candle

Paper

Begin by lighting the red candle, symbolizing action, energy, and determination. Write your goal or intention clearly on the piece of paper. Fold this paper and place it at the bottom of the jar, setting the foundation for your manifestation.

Add a pinch of graveyard dirt into the jar. Graveyard dirt is often used in spells to symbolize the finality of transformation and the power of renewal. It helps in grounding your goal and giving it a solid foundation.

Next, sprinkle some pepper into the jar. Pepper is used for its fiery energy, symbolizing the speed and force with which you want your goals to be realized. It's also believed to ward off negativity or obstacles that may hinder your path to success.

As you add each ingredient, visualize your goal being charged with energy and coming to fruition. Focus on the feelings of achievement and the positive changes it will bring into your life.

Once all the ingredients are in the jar, seal it with its lid or cork. Hold the jar in your hands as you sit quietly, focusing on your goal. Visualize a bright light surrounding the jar, charging it with even more energy. Repeat the following affirmation:

"With these elements, I set my course,
Dirt for grounding, pepper for force.
This candle's flame ignites my desire,
With every flicker, I'm lifted higher.
Sealed in this jar, my intention is set,
My goal is clear, my ambition met."

Extinguish the candle to conclude the ritual. Place the jar in a space where you will see it often, serving as a constant reminder of your goal and the energies working towards its accomplishment. Whenever you feel the need, hold the jar and reaffirm your intention, visualizing your goal as already achieved.

Home Protection Crystal Enchantment

You will need:

Large Crystal

Large Bowl or Cauldron

Water

Sea Salt

Basil

Something from your home/yard

Wand or something to stir the water

Place your crystal in the cauldron and fill it with enough water to cover the crystal. Throw a pinch of salt into the cauldron and say the following:

"Bless this family and bless this home,
When we're here and when we roam,
When darkness beckons our light will shine,
And protect the ones that I call mine."

Throw in a pinch of basil and something from your yard or home, it can be a rock, a leaf, a blade a grass or even a fiber from your carpet, it just needs to be something that has a connection to the property you are blessing.

Use your wand to stir the water in a clockwise motion, do 7 complete circles around the crystal while stirring.

Display the crystal in a common area of the home.

Confidence Tea Ritual

This is a simple morning tea ritual to get that positive energy flowing and to set our intentions for the day.

You will need:

Your favorite type of tea

Your favorite teacup

Simply boil the tea and pour into your favorite cup and say the following:

*"Confident, beautiful, secure and grand,
I hold the future in the palm of my hand,
I'll conquer the day and reap the rewards,
While always moving forever forwards."*

Relax and drink your tea while thinking of all the things you're going to accomplish today.

Clairvoyance Ritual

This ritual is designed to enhance clairvoyance – the ability to see through illusions and deceptions – by seeking the blessing of Veritas, the goddess of truth.

You will need:

A small mirror

A quiet, undisturbed space

Begin by finding a peaceful area where you can focus without interruptions. Cleanse the space and yourself to ensure the energy is pure. This can be done using incense, sage, or simply by setting a clear, calm intention.

Place the mirror before you, ensuring it is clean and unobstructed. The mirror acts as a symbolic gateway to clarity and truth, aiding in your quest for clairvoyance.

Center yourself with a few deep breaths, grounding your energy and clearing your mind. When you feel ready, focus your gaze into the mirror, allowing your eyes to relax. It's not about looking at your reflection, but rather looking through it, as if peering into another realm.

Call upon Veritas with the following invocation:

"Veritas, goddess of truth and clarity,
I seek your blessing in this sacred mirror.
Grant me the vision to see through illusion,
To discern truth amidst confusion.
May your light guide me to clear sight,
Revealing what's hidden in plain sight."

Continue to gaze into the mirror, letting your mind open to any images, symbols, or feelings that arise. The mirror, combined with your invocation, becomes a conduit for Veritas's energy and wisdom.

After the ritual, thank Veritas for her guidance and blessing. To maintain and strengthen your clairvoyance, it's important to regularly show adoration to Veritas. This can be done by making small offerings – such as burning a candle or incense in her honor, placing a glass of water on your altar, or simply spending a few moments each day in gratitude, acknowledging her continued assistance. These acts of devotion will help sustain the power of clairvoyance she bestows upon you and maintain your connection to this wonderful goddess of Truth.

To Bless a Relationship

A simple ritual to do with your significant other to ensure a long lasting and happy relationship.

You will need:
Loaf of Bread
Wine Glass
Othala Rune

Bake a fresh loaf of bread. Hold it up to the moon and ask the gods and goddesses to bless the bread as well as the relationship. Break off a piece of the bread for your partner, as well as one for yourself as well and fill the glass you'll be sharing with any beverage of your choice.

Incorporate the Othala Rune in any way you'd like, you can etch or draw it onto the wine glass, bake it into the bread design or simply draw it on a piece of paper and use it as a coaster for the glass.

As you share time together, share the bread as well. Do not cut the bread with a knife or any other cutting tool. Just break off the pieces with your hands. The bread may be any type you like, you can add butter, jam, or anything else that you and your partner might like.

New Moon Blessings

New Moon Ritual for Hecate's Blessings

This ritual is designed to honor Hecate, the goddess of magic and crossroads during the new moon, seeking her guidance and blessings for the upcoming lunar cycle.

You will need:
A black candle
An obsidian stone
A key
A black ribbon

Begin by creating a sacred space where you can perform the ritual undisturbed. Place the black candle in the center of your space and arrange the obsidian stone and the key nearby. The black candle represents the dark moon and Hecate's mysteries, the obsidian for grounding and protection, and the key symbolizes unlocking wisdom and opportunities.

Light the black candle to signify the start of the ritual and to invoke Hecate's presence. Hold the obsidian stone in your hand, feeling its energy grounding you, connecting you to the earth and to Hecate's liminal realm.

Focus on the new moon, a time of new beginnings and potential. Reflect on what you wish to manifest or release during this lunar cycle. With these intentions in mind, tie the black ribbon around the key while saying:

"Hecate, ancient goddess of the night and crossroads, I call upon you in this sacred hour of the new moon.

With this key, I seek your wisdom and strength, to unlock the mysteries and opportunities that lie ahead in this lunar cycle.

I bind this ribbon as a symbol of your enduring guidance and protection.

May your insight illuminate my path, and your blessings be upon me as I journey through the coming month."

Visualize Hecate's energy imbuing the key with her power and wisdom. Feel her presence as a guiding force in the upcoming lunar cycle. The key, now tied with the black ribbon, symbolizes your connection to Hecate and her blessings.

Extinguish the candle to mark the end of the ritual. Keep the key with you throughout the month as a reminder of Hecate's blessings and guidance. Each time you see or touch the key remember the intentions set during this new moon and feel empowered by Hecate's presence in your journey.

Calming Spell

This ritual is designed to provide a sense of calm and tranquility without the need for any physical ritual items. It centers around a soothing mantra that invokes the goddess's gift of peace.

Begin by taking a few deep, slow breaths to center yourself. With each inhale, draw in serenity and with each exhale, release any tension or stress you may be carrying.

Once you feel centered, open your palms and gaze softly into them. Palms are often seen as personal and powerful symbols of connection and receptivity. As you look into your palms, repeat the following mantra gently, either out loud or in your mind:

"As I look into my palm,
The goddess grants the gift of calm."

As you recite these words, visualize a gentle, soothing energy flowing from the universe, through your palms, and into your entire being. Imagine this energy as a light or a warm sensation, bringing with it peace and tranquility that fills your body and mind.

Continue to repeat the mantra as many times as you feel necessary. With each repetition, allow yourself to sink deeper into a state of calm and relaxation. Feel the presence of the goddess enveloping you in a protective and peaceful embrace.

When you feel sufficiently calmed and grounded, slowly cease the repetition of the mantra. Take a few more deep breaths, expressing silent gratitude to the goddess for her gift of calm. Gently bring your awareness back to your surroundings.

This ritual can be performed anytime you feel the need for peace and serenity. It's a simple yet powerful tool to restore balance and calm in your life.

Guiding Light Meditation

This is a calming meditation ritual to seek guidance and clarity from your inner light.

You will need:
A comfortable meditation cushion
A small mirror
A blue candle

Light the blue candle and sit comfortably on the meditation cushion. Hold the mirror in front of you and gaze into it, allowing your mind to calm and your thoughts to still. Focus on the candle's flame reflected in the mirror and imagine it as a beacon of internal wisdom. Recite softly:

"Inner light, so bright and clear,
Guide my thoughts, bring insight near.
In this flame, the truth I see,
My path revealed, set my spirit free."

Continue to meditate, letting the light from the candle guide your thoughts towards clarity and understanding. When you feel ready, extinguish the candle and reflect on any insights you received.

Remove Curse From an Object

This ritual focuses on removing a curse from an object using the purifying properties of sage and saltwater. It is a gentle yet effective method to cleanse and neutralize negative energies.

You will need:

The cursed object

A bowl of saltwater (preferably sea salt dissolved in water)

A white candle

A sage smudging stick

A piece of black cloth

Begin by selecting a quiet, peaceful location where you won't be disturbed. This environment is crucial for maintaining focus and intent during the ritual.

Light the white candle to symbolize purity, light, and positive energy. The flame acts as a beacon of cleansing and protection.

Light the sage smudging stick, allowing the smoke to waft around the cursed object. Sage is renowned for its cleansing properties and is believed to banish negative energies. As you smudge the area, you can say a simple invocation or prayer for cleansing, such as, "With this sage, I cleanse this object of all negative energies and curses, restoring balance and peace."

Dip your fingers into the bowl of saltwater. Saltwater is traditionally used for purification and grounding. Gently sprinkle the saltwater over the cursed object. As you do this, envision the water drawing out the curse, neutralizing and washing away any negativity attached to the item.

Once you have sufficiently sprinkled the object with saltwater, wrap it in the black cloth. The black cloth acts as a barrier, absorbing any residual negative energy. Leave the object wrapped for a period of time — this could be a few hours to a full day, depending on your intuition and the perceived strength of the curse.

To conclude the ritual, unwrap the object and safely extinguish the candle and sage.

Healing from a Past Relationship

This is a ritual for healing a broken heart, ending a dying relationship and starting anew. Do this spell under a full or new moon.

Call upon your goddess/god of choice and say the following chant until you feel the pain lift from your heart.

"Oh Goddess, take my pain
steady as a falling rain.
Give me courage to call an end,
give me a chance to start again.
Help heal all the broken hearts,
So that we may easily part.
Oh, Goddess let my will be done,
with no harm to anyone.
Blessed Be! So mote it be!"

Visualize yourself in your mind, happy, ending with ease and starting new and fresh. See new beginnings and happy times ahead for you with no more pain.

Healing a Broken Heart

This ritual is designed for anyone experiencing heartache, providing a gentle, nurturing process to aid in emotional healing. It's versatile, suitable for various causes of heartbreak.

You will need:

A small bag or pouch

Rose petals

A pink rose quartz heart (optional)

Begin by finding a quiet, comfortable space where you can be undisturbed. This ritual is best performed in a peaceful environment where you feel safe and relaxed.

As you prepare to start, take a few deep breaths. With each inhale, imagine drawing in calm and healing energy; with each exhale, release the pain and sorrow from your heart.

Take the rose petals and, one by one, place them into the small bag. As you do this, think of each petal representing a step towards healing. Roses are traditionally associated with love and healing, and their presence in this ritual helps to gently soothe and mend a broken heart.

If you have a pink rose quartz heart, hold it in your hands for a moment. Feel its smooth surface and gentle energy. Rose quartz is known for its properties of love and emotional healing. Place the quartz heart in the bag with the rose petals.

Once you have filled the bag, hold it in your hands and close your eyes. Visualize a soft, nurturing light surrounding you, offering comfort and strength. Say the following (either aloud or in your mind):

"Healing light, gentle and true,
Guide my heart to renew.
With these petals and quartz so near,
Let my heart heal, free from fear.
As I carry this bag, let it be a sign,
Of the healing journey that is rightfully mine."

Keep the bag with you as a reminder of your commitment to healing. It serves as a talisman of love and self-care. Whenever you feel overwhelmed, hold the bag, and remember the healing intentions you've set.

Keep the bag close until you feel your heart has mended. The time needed for this process varies for everyone and it's okay to take as long as you need. When you feel ready and your heart feels whole again, you can return the rose petals to the earth as a symbol of gratitude and release the energy back into the universe. If you used a rose quartz heart, you may keep it as a personal healing stone or place it in a special space as a reminder of your resilience and strength.

Moonlight Purification Ritual

This ritual is designed to cleanse and purify your space using the gentle energy of the moonlight.

You will need:
A small bowl of water
A white candle
A piece of clear quartz

Begin by lighting the white candle and placing the bowl of water in front of you. Hold the clear quartz in your hand and visualize it absorbing the moon's energy. Gently swirl the water with the quartz, envisioning the moon's light purifying the water. As you do this, softly chant:

"By the moon's gracious light,
Cleanse this space, make it bright.
With quartz so clear and water pure,
In this space, good energies endure."

Allow the candle to burn down safely and leave the bowl of water under the moonlight overnight. The next morning, use the water to anoint doorways and windows, infusing your space with purified energy.

To Prevent Nightmares

You will need:

White Candles

Spoon of Mint Leaves or Mint Tea

Hot Water

1 Glass

Put the Spearmint Leaves into the glass and add the hot water, you can use a tea infuser if you'd like.

Place the three candles in a triangle around the glass, light the candles and say the following.

"I am safe while I sleep, there is nothing to fear.
for now I understand, nothing can hurt me in here."

Blow out the candles and take a sip of the tea. At first a daily ritual before bedtime is recommended. After a few days try extending the time between days you need to perform the ritual until the nightmares are completely gone and the ritual is no longer necessary.

Garden Growth Spell

Elemental Garden Blessing Ritual

This ritual is designed to enrich and protect your garden by invoking the elemental forces of nature, using a crystal or stone, seashell, feather, and cinnamon stick as representatives.

You will need:

A crystal/stone for Earth
A seashell for Water
A feather for Air
Cinnamon for Fire
A handful of earth from your garden

Arrange the stone, seashell, feather, and cinnamon stick in a circle around you in your garden, creating a sacred space. These items symbolize the connection to the Earth, the flow of Water, the breath of Air, and the energy of Fire, respectively.

Hold the handful of earth from your garden and feel its connection to the natural world. As you stand within your circle of elemental representations, focus your intent on nurturing and protecting your garden.

With the earth in your hands, begin to gently spread it around your garden. As you do so, recite the following mantra:

"Elements of nature, graceful and strong,
Bless this garden, as days grow long.
Earth grounds, Water flows,
Air breathes, and Fire glows.
Together in harmony, your powers I call,
To protect and nourish, one and all.
With this Earth I spread,
May spirit and matter be fed."

Visualize each element bestowing its unique gifts upon your garden. Imagine the earth providing a strong foundation, water offering life-giving moisture, air delivering vital oxygen, and fire imparting growth and energy.

Continue to walk through your garden, spreading the rest of the earth, allowing the words and your actions to infuse the space with positive energy and protection. Feel the presence of the elemental forces surrounding your garden, encouraging growth, health, and vitality. Give thanks to the Elementals of your garden to conclude the ritual. You may collect the ritual items or leave them in your garden.

Third Eye Ritual

This ritual is designed to activate and enhance the power of your third eye, using the natural energies of an Amethyst stone, incense, and a purple candle. Regular practice of this ritual can progressively strengthen your intuitive abilities.

You will need:

Amethyst stone

Incense

Purple candle

Start by finding a quiet space where you can sit comfortably without distractions. Place the Amethyst stone in front of you, light the incense, and then light the purple candle. The purple color of the candle resonates with the third eye chakra, aiding in its activation, while the scent of the incense helps to calm your mind and prepare you for deeper intuitive work.

Hold the Amethyst stone in your hands and close your eyes. Take deep, slow breaths, allowing the incense's aroma to fill your senses. Visualize the purple light of the candle merging with the energy of the Amethyst, creating a radiant, indigo light.

Focus your attention on the area between your eyebrows, where the third eye chakra is located. Imagine this indigo light from the Amethyst and the candle flame entering your third eye, activating and opening it. As you breathe in, feel the light expanding, and as you breathe out, release any blockages or doubts.

Continue to meditate with the Amethyst, allowing its energy to work in tandem with the candlelight and incense, enhancing your third eye chakra. When you feel the session is complete, gently open your eyes and extinguish the candle. It's recommended to perform this ritual regularly, especially during moments of self-reflection or when seeking deeper understanding, to further advance the power and sensitivity of your third eye.

Crafting Your Own Rituals

A ritual can be anything you imagine that aids you in bringing about changes in the world that you wish to see. Rituals can also be used to revere and honor the spirits, gods and goddesses.

Rituals are usually proceeded by a circle casting, the practitioner can use tools to gather, disperse, and direct energies for the purposes of manifestation, which means to bring about some sort of change thru use of magic.

The tools used in your rituals are there to aid you in setting and focusing your intentions to properly channel the energies being used to bring about change you wish to see.

There's no right or wrong way to conduct a ritual, your primary concern and the reason we use tools and circles is to prevent an accidental misdirection of your intentions which could lead to a failure in your goals or in the case of darker magic, like binding spells, potential harm upon an unintended target.

When conducting "white magic" rituals there's little risk to the caster or anyone involved and the worst that can happen is a possible energy drain that could be accompanied by headaches and fatigue. So, rituals for protection, confidence, worship, and self-empowerment are a great starting point for someone learning to craft their own rituals and spells.

In Closing

I hope you enjoyed my ritual book! The world of magic is vast and there is a seemingly limitless wealth of information on countless topics so let this book be a steppingstone on your own spiritual path.

In my own spiritual journey, I've been inspired by countless cultures and practices, the ancient writings of Greek and Roman pagans, tales of the Norse gods, the Marian devotion of Catholicism, the profound and enlightening poetry and story-telling of Hinduism and Buddhism, and the ancient wisdom of Hebrew mystic traditions. Our history as practitioners of magic is intertwined with the development of a multitude of ancient practices, and it is in this tapestry of faiths that we find the threads of universal truth connecting us all that is meant to bring us all together.

By exploring the knowledge and wisdom of various spiritual practices, you can gain a deeper understanding of the underlying spiritual truths that transcend any single belief system. Just as different rivers eventually merge into the same vast ocean, so too can the diverse faiths of the world lead us to a greater comprehension of the spiritual essence that unites us all. Attend a Catholic Mass, visit a Mosque or Jewish Community center, speak with a Hindu priest or devotee, and seek out a community of people that are also open minded and seeking wisdom.

May your journey for spiritual enlightenment be boundless, your curiosity insatiable, and your heart open to the profound wisdom that can be found through knowledge of the past and an understanding of the present. As you continue to walk your path, remember that the quest for knowledge is a never-ending adventure without limitation, and your pursuit of the sacred will forever lead you toward the light of understanding, don't be afraid to leave your comfort zone and don't be afraid of failure.

If you have a moment, please leave a book review! I self-publish all my books and it really helps as I don't have any publishers out there pushing my content. Thank you for reading my book and blessed be!

Merry met!
And merry part!
-Brittany Nightshade-

Disclaimer: Always take safety precautions when doing any ritual. Be careful if using stoves or any heat sources. This information is educational and religious and is not to be taken as professional medical advice. Use this book at your own peril, I'm not responsible for any unintended consequences. never ingest anything unless you're completely sure it's safe, you have been fully warned. Do not commit any crimes, such as trespassing, when conducting your rituals...I don't have a spell to get you out of jail.

Much Love, Brittany

If you've enjoyed the book, please consider giving me a review on and following me on Instagram and Facebook.

facebook.com/xobrittanynightshade

@BrittanyNightshadeOfficial